T0020928

LAUGH
-Out-
LOUD

TRY NOT TO LOL

JOKES
for KIDS

LAUGH
-Out-
LOUD
TRY NOT TO LOL

JOKES
for KIDS

ROB ELLIOTT

Library of Congress Control Number: 2020952877
ISBN 978-0-06-299189-8

21 22 23 24 25   PC/BRR   10 9 8 7 6 5 4 3
❖
First Edition

As an adoptive dad, I'd like to dedicate this book to the kids who are experiencing the challenges of foster care and the families who care for them. May you be blessed with laughter, love, and the gift of family!

—R. E.

Q: What do you get when you combine a cat, a skunk, and a clown?

A: A cat that smells funny.

Q: Why did the tennis players get in trouble?

A: They were making too much racquet.

Q: What do you call a creative fish?

A: Minnow-vative!

Q: Why don't polar bears live in Australia?

A: They don't koala-fy.

HA HA
HA HA

- - - - - - - - - - - - - - - - - -

Q: What kind of tears do cowboys cry?

A: Frontiers.

Q: What do you call a comedian with a cup of grape juice?

A: Enter-staining!

Q: Did you hear about the guy who was caught stealing a calendar?

A: The judge gave him twelve months!

Q: What do boxers have at their birthday party?

A: Pound cake and punch!

Q: **What do you call a cheerful wizard?**

A: Opti-mystic.

Q: **What does a race car driver wear to the beach?**

A: A Lambor-kini.

Q: **What kind of monster might you find in the woods in Russia?**

A: A Nyet-i!

Q: What is the difference between a sheep and a sheep dog?

A: One has fleece and the other has fleas.

Knock, knock.

Who's there?

Chicken.

Chicken who?

Just chicken to see if you're home.

Q: **What happens when you bring your teacher a biscuit?**

A: She'll put you on the honor roll.

Q: **What's a housekeeper's favorite dessert?**

A: Sponge cake.

Q: **What do you get when you cross meat, potatoes, and a dictionary?**

A: Something stew-dious.

Phil: How do I tell my mom I don't like her hot dogs?

Will: Just be frank.

Q: What do horses put on their pancakes?

A: Butter and stirrup.

Q: How many letters are in the alphabet if you take out the *a* and the *e*?

A: Six! There are eight letters in the word .

Q: What did the kids say when the carnival left town?

A: That's so un-fair!

Q: Why can't you trust a flight of stairs?

A: They're always up to something.

Q: How did the race car driver feel after the race was over?

A: Exhaust-ed!

Q: Why did they evacuate the baseball stadium?

A: There were too many bats!

Q: What is a bird's favorite kind of treat?

A: Chocolate chirp cookies.

Q: Who is the quietest fish in the sea?

A: The great white shhhhhhark.

Q: What's an Alaskan husky's favorite kind of vegetable?

A: Mush-rooms!

Q: What do bubble gum and a train have in common?

A: They both chew, chew, chew.

Knock, knock.

Who's there?

Dallas.

Dallas who?

This is Dallas straw!

Q: Why did Jupiter break up with Pluto?

A: It needed some space.

Q: Why did the young skunk get in trouble with his mom?

A: He should have had the scents to know better.

Knock, knock.

Who's there?

August.

August who?

August of wind blew my hat off.

Knock, knock.

Who's there?

Dale.

Dale who?

Dale be consequences if you don't open the door!

Knock, knock.

Who's there?

Gwen.

Gwen who?

Gwen do you think you'll get around to opening the door?

Q: What is the great thing about elevator jokes?

A: They are funny on so many levels!

Knock, knock.

Who's there?

Earl and Bert.

Earl and Bert who?

The Earl and Bert gets the worm.

Q: Why are spices so trustworthy?

A: They're always on thyme.

Q: What kind of snack can you eat in the library?

A: Hush puppies.

Q: What do a kitten and a baker have in common?

A: They both like to start from scratch.

Q: How does a farmer count his animals in the barn?

A: He uses a cow-culator.

HA HA
HA HA

Q: Why did King Kong climb to the top of the Empire State Building?

A: He was too big to fit in the elevator!

Q: What do you get when you cross a dentist and a band director?

A: A tuba toothpaste.

Q: Why do mathematicians make good friends?

A: Because you can always count on them.

Q: Why did the deer go shopping for pants?

A: Because it was buck naked!

Q: Why did the pig get kicked out of the soccer game?

A: Because it was hogging the ball.

Knock, knock.

Who's there?

Ostrich.

Ostrich who?

Ostrich my legs before I go for a run.

Q: **What kind of shoes do art teachers wear?**

A: Skechers.

Q: **What do you call a squirrel in a space suit?**

A: An astro-nut.

Q: **What do you call a kitten that likes to bowl?**

A: An alley cat.

Q: **What kind of vegetable will put you in a good mood?**

A: Hap-peas!

Q: What is the number-one game in the world?

A: Uno!

Knock, knock.

Who's there?

Kelp.

Kelp who?

Kelp me open the door.

Q: Why did the computer go to the doctor?

A: It was losing its memory.

Knock, knock.

Who's there?

Otter.

Otter who?

You otter open up so I can tell you another joke!

Q: Why did the boy bring a can of soda to class?

A: He heard there might be a pop quiz!

Q: Why did the dinosaur go to the gas station?

A: It wanted some fossil fuel.

Q: What do you get when you combine a skunk and a dinosaur?

A: A stink-a-saurus.

Q: What did the whale say to the beach?

A: Long time no sea.

Q: What do you call a dog who's the life of the party?

A: Pup-ular!

Q: What do you hear when you cross a witch and a race car?

A: Broom, broom, broom ...

Q: Why did the duck refuse to take its medicine?

A: It thought the doctor was a quack.

Knock, knock.

Who's there?

Window.

Window who?

Window you want to hear another joke?

- -

Q: How do hot dogs feel about taking a vacation?

A: They relish it!

Knock, knock.

Who's there?

Olive.

Olive who?

Olive to tell you all my jokes.

Q: What is a fish's favorite kind of music?

A: Christmas corals.

Q: Why do pine trees get straight As in math class?

A: They know all about geome-tree and square roots.

Q: Why do potatoes always win at hide and seek?

A: They keep their eyes peeled.

Q: What is the smartest bug in the world?

A: The spelling bee.

Q: Why did the astronaut get bad grades in school?

A: He was always spacing out!

Q: Why did Dracula's flashlight go out?

A: It had a low bat-tery.

Q: Why don't mummies get invited to parties?

A: They get a bad wrap.

Q: **What is the smartest dinosaur in the world?**

A: The thesaurus.

Q: **Why couldn't the electrician go to sleep?**

A: He was wired.

Q: **What is a whale's favorite game?**

A: Go Fish.

Q: **What color is the wind?**

A: Blew.

Q: Why did the frog go out for breakfast?

A: His toad-ster was broken.

Q: Why did the triangle go to the gym?

A: To stay in shape!

Q: What is a lizard's favorite game?

A: Cricket.

Q: How do fleas get from one dog to another?

A: They itch-hike.

Q: What do barbers and race car drivers have in common?

A: They both like short cuts.

Q: How do cows do their Christmas shopping?

A: From a cattle-log.

Q: How do sheep celebrate the Fourth of July?

A: They have a baa-baa-cue.

Q: What do you call a king who's only twelve inches tall?

A: The ruler!

Student: I finished writing my paper about honey.

Teacher: I give it a bee!

Q: What kind of drink is always missing?

A: Absen-tea.

Knock, knock.

Who's there?

Waiter.

Waiter who?

Waiter minute and I'll tell you another knock-knock joke.

HA HA
HA HA

George: Did you hear my joke about paper?

Jon: I did, and it was tear-able!

Q: Why did the teacher get glasses?

A: Because she couldn't control her pupils.

Q: What kind of creatures come out during a storm?

A: Lightning bugs.

Q: Why can't a T. Rex clap its hands?

A: Because it's extinct!

- -

Q: Why did the farmer keep a rooster by his bed?

A: He needed an alarm cluck!

Q: Why did the peanut go out with the raisin?

A: Because it couldn't find a date.

Q: Why did the man start to cry when he hit a nail with a hammer?

A: It was his finger-nail!

Q: Why couldn't the pony sing a song?

A: Because it was a little hoarse.

Q: Why did the snowman cancel his date?

A: He got cold feet!

Q: Why was the parrot feeling embarrassed?

A: It saw the pirate's booty.

- -

Knock, knock.

Who's there?

Yukon.

Yukon who?

Yukon come out and play anytime!

Knock, knock.

Who's there?

Wheelie.

Wheelie who?

I wheelie want you to open the door!

Knock, knock.

Who's there?

Kitten.

Kitten who?

Just kitten, I don't really want to come in.

Q: What did the baker do on vacation?

A: She just loafed around.

Q: Why wouldn't the basketball player get on the bus?

A: The ref said traveling was against the rules.

Q: How do musicians drink their lemonade?

A: With an orche-straw.

Q: What do you call a funny chicken?

A: A comedi-hen.

Q: Why can't you trust train conductors?

A: They have loco-motives!

Q: Where do you keep your gold on St. Patrick's Day?

A: In a lepre-can!

Knock, knock.

Who's there?

Treble.

Treble who?

Is it too much treble to open the door?

Q: Why won't chicks ever buy you a present?

A: Because they're cheep, cheep, cheep.

Marley: Can I trade you a dollar for ninety-nine pennies?

Mickey: That doesn't make cents!

Jane: Hey, did I tell you the joke about my laundry?

Dan: No, I only want to hear a clean joke.

Q: What do you call a philosopher in a scuba suit?

A: A deep-sea diver.

Q: When is a baker too greedy?

A: When he keeps all the dough to himself.

Q: What is the dumbest animal in the jungle?

A: A polar bear!

Q: **Why do pilots miss so many days of work?**

A: They're always getting the flew.

Knock, knock.

Who's there?

Minnow.

Minnow who?

Let minnow if you want to hear another joke.

Q: **Where do cows keep their pictures?**

A: On their bull-etin board.

Q: Why did the vampire become a vegetarian?

A: He hated stakes!

Jake: Have you ever seen a fish bowl?

Zac: No, but I've seen a frog jump.

Q: How many skunks does it take to stink up your house?

A: A phew!

Q: Why was the little boy planting flowers?

A: He was a kinder-gardener.

Q: Why are pancakes cooler than waffles?

A: Because waffles are square.

Q: Why do you want turkeys in your marching band?

A: Because they'll always have their drumsticks with them!

Q: Why did the pie go to the dentist?

A: It needed its filling.

Q: What do you do if they run out of umbrellas at the store?

A: Ask for a raincheck.

Q: How do snowmen call their friends?

A: On a snow-mobile.

Q: What does Jack Frost's wife put on her face at night?

A: Cold cream.

Knock, knock.

Who's there?

Toad.

Toad who?

Have I toad you lately that I love you?

HA HA
HA HA

Q: Why should you invite hockey players to all your parties?

A: They know how to break the ice.

Q: Why did the strawberry call 911?

A: It was in a jam.

Q: Why did the Milk Dud go to school?

A: It wanted to be like the Smarties.

Q: Why was the rabbit feeling embarrassed?

A: It was having a bad hare day!

Q: What do you give an elephant that can't fall asleep?

A: A trunk-quilizer.

Q: Where do fish take naps?

A: In their riverbeds.

Q: What does a pine tree do on a chilly day?

A: It puts on its fir coat.

Knock, knock.

Who's there?

Douglas.

Douglas who?

Douglas is only half full.

Q: What is a skunk's favorite game?

A: Hide and reek.

Q: Why couldn't the pig write a letter

to its friend?

A: Its pen ran out of oink.

Knock, knock.

Who's there?

Goat.

Goat who?

You've goat to be kidding me!

Q: Why did the rabbit get a new job?

A: It was looking for new hopper-

tunities.

Q: What do trees do to get ready for

company?

A: They spruce things up.

Q: What's the worst blood type to have if you're an author?

A: Typ-o.

Q: Why was the miner in pain?

A: He got a coal sore.

Millie: What do you get a scarecrow for his birthday?

Quincy: Well, that's a no-brainer!

- -

Knock, knock.

Who's there?

Figs.

Figs who?

Figs the doorbell so I don't have to knock!

Q: What do you call a guy with an empty wallet and a can of beans?

A: Desti-toot!

Q: What is the most spiritual kind of animal?

A: A chip-monk.

Q: Why are fireflies so cheerful?

A: They always look on the bright side.

Q: Why did the man quit his job as a banker?

A: He lost interest!

Knock, knock.

Who's there?

Panther.

Panther who?

Watch out—your panther falling down!

Knock, knock.

Who's there?

Freddie.

Freddie who?

Freddie or not, here I come!

Q: What did the meatball say to the spaghetti?

A: You seem stretched too thin!

Q: Why did the panda go off its diet?

A: It couldn't bear it anymore!

Q: Why do whales make good roommates?

A: Because they're so tide-y.

Q: **What does Cupid put on his burns?**

A: An-gel.

Q: **Why can't you trust a sheep?**

A: They'll pull the wool over your eyes.

Q: **What do you call a lazy cow?**

A: Meat-loaf.

Q: **What is the easiest kind of lid to open?**

A: Your eyelid!

Josh: I got hit in the head with can of soda pop yesterday.

Justin: Oh no, did it hurt?

Josh: No, it was a soft drink.

Q: What do you get when you cross a chicken and a barista?

A: A coffee rooster.

Q: Why are bakers so classy?

A: They're always well-bread.

Q: Why do penguins like to hang out together?

A: To keep from feeling ice-olated.

Q: Why are chefs so mean in the kitchen?

A: They beat their eggs and whip their butter!

Q: What does a Jedi like to drive?

A: A Toy-yoda.

Q: Why did the koala have to get a job?

A: Because it was bear-oke!

Q: Why did the cowboy's horse start to sneeze?

A: It had hay fever.

Q: What did the teacher do on the last day of school?

A: She did a summer-sault!

Q: Where will you find a zombie's house?

A: On a dead-end street.

Knock, knock.

Who's there?

Doris.

Doris who?

If the Doris open, I'll come on in.

Knock, knock.

Who's there?

Delia.

Delia who?

**If I Delia some cards, we can play Go
Fish.**

Q: Why was the dentist crying?

A: A patient hurt his fillings.

Q: What do you call angry broccoli?

A: Steamed veggies!

Knock, knock.

Who's there?

Buttermilk.

Buttermilk who?

You buttermilk the cows on time!

Q: Why don't bananas get lonely?

A: They like to hang out in bunches.

HA HA
HA HA

Q: How is a beekeeper like poison ivy?

A: They'll both give you hives.

Q: Why did the vampire go to the doctor?

A: He was tired of the coffin.

Q: What is a baseball player's favorite dessert?

A: Bunt cake with a pitcher of milk.

Q: How do alligators cook their food?

A: They use a croc-pot.

Q: What is a chicken's favorite vegetable?

A: They like eggplant!

Q: Why did the English teacher go to jail?

A: The judge gave him a really tough sentence.

Q: Where does a cat go hiking?

A: In the meow-ntains.

Knock, knock.

Who's there?

Ida.

Ida who?

No, it's pronounced Idaho.

Q: What happened when the dinosaurs crashed into each other?

A: It was a tyrannosaurus wreck!

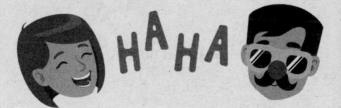

Q: Did you hear about the noodle that went down the drain?

A: It pasta way!

Q: Why did the deer get a job?

A: Because it was out of doe.

Q: What did the attorney wear to work?

A: A lawsuit.

Knock, knock.

Who's there?

Anita.

Anita who?

Anita key to open the door!

Q: **How did the chickens get out of the coop?**

A: They used the eggs-it.

Q: **Why did the lumberjacks stay in bed all day?**

A: Because they were sawing logs.

Q: **How much does it cost to swim with the sharks?**

A: An arm and a leg!

Q: **What kind of paper does a builder use?**

A: Construction paper.

Q: **Why are cheaters so bad at spelling?**

A: Because they're always breaking their word.

Q: **Why can you trust a walrus with your secrets?**

A: Their lips are always seal-ed!

Q: **How did the farmer become a millionaire?**

A: She knew how to bring home the bacon!

Q: How do you keep a rhinoceros from charging?

A: Take away its batteries.

Leah: Did you read that book about Mount Everest?

Anna: No, just summit up for me.

Q: Why did the soccer players fall in love?

A: They got a kick out of each other.

Q: Why did the bear eat the light bulb?

A: It wanted a light snack.

Q: Why did the writer run around the block?

A: He had all that penned-up energy!

Mario: Did you know that an alligator can eat two people at once?

Mason: I think that's a croc!

Sam: My job is so easy, I can do it in my sleep.

Marcus: Wow, that sounds like a dream job!

Bess: Can you think of any good jokes about trees?

Kris: Nope, I'm stumped.

Q: What do you call a crocodile with a good sense of direction?

A: A navi-gator.

Q: Why did the man give up hunting?

A: He said it was for the birds!

Q: What do you call a bug that never leaves?

A: Perman-ant.

Q: Why did the cucumber yell for help?

A: It was in a pickle.

Knock, knock.

Who's there?

Joanna.

Joanna who?

Joanna let me in or not?

Q: What did the hammer say to the saw?

A: You're looking sharp.

Q: How many chickens does it take to make a pot of soup?

A: None—chickens can't cook.

Q: Why was the wasp nervous on its first day of school?

A: Because it was a new-bee.

Q: How do astronauts wash their hair?

A: They take meteor showers.

Q: Why did the cow need a razor?

A: To shave its moo-stache.

Q: Where does a kangaroo like to go for breakfast?

A: IHOP!

Q: Why did the baseball player go to the doctor?

A: He was catching something.

Q: Why was the pickle late for school?

A: It was dill-y-dallying.

HA HA
HA HA

Q: What do you call a sleepy landscaper?

A: A yawn mower.

Q: Why can't a cannon hold a job?

A: It's always getting fired.

Q: Why was the fisherman dancing?

A: He heard a catchy tuna.

Knock, knock.

Who's there?

Moron.

Moron who?

There's moron the subject if you want to hear about it.

Q: What is the meanest animal in the swamp?

A: A bully-frog!

Q: Why did the fish go on a diet?

A: It checked its scales.

Q: What do you call a musical snake?

A: A boa conductor.

Q: Why did the cactus put on a tuxedo?

A: It wanted to look sharp!

Q: Why did the plate lie to the bowl?

A: It was dish-honest.

Q: What do bats eat for breakfast?

A: Flapjacks.

Q: What do dogs eat for breakfast?

A: Woof-les.

Q: What did the golden retriever say to the poodle?

A: I've got a bone to pick with you!

Q: What happens if a bee flies up your nose?

A: It ticklezzzzz.

Q: What's a whale's favorite snack?

A: Blubber gum.

Q: What do golfers like to drink?

A: Iced tee!

Q: What kind of animal never has any money?

A: A poor-cupine.

Q: What kind of shoes do plumbers wear?

A: Clogs.

Q: What kind of car does a dog drive?

A: A station waggin'.

Q: What do you get if you cross a snail and a camera?

A: Shell-fies.

Q: What do you call a kangaroo that just sits around?

A: A pouch potato.

Q: What's a porcupine's favorite hobby?

A: Quill-ting.

Q: How did the bird get across the lake?

A: In a crow-boat.

Q: Why was the policeman snoring?

A: He had gone undercover.

Q: How do you take a sheep to the hospital?

A: In a lamb-ulance!

Q: What is the best thing to drink at a parade?

A: A root beer float.

Q: What do you call a frog that never tells the truth?

A: An am-fib-ian.

Q: Why is a baker like the internet?

A: They'll both give you cookies.

Q: What do you call a cow that goes to the gym?

A: A buff-alo.

Q: What do you call a monster who gets straight As?

A: An ogre-achiever!

Q: Why did the maple tree send a valentine?

A: It was being sappy.

Q: What do you eat in a kayak?

A: Float-meal.

Q: Why is a train like a tattletale?

A: They'll both blow the whistle on you.

Q: What did the cowboy say when he fell off his horse?

A: Help! I've fallen and I can't giddyup!

Q: Why were wristwatches invented?

A: So people would have more time on their hands.

Q: Why was the shark embarrassed?

A: Because it saw the ocean's bottom.

Q: What do you get when you combine a dog and a cow?

A: Hound beef.

Q: What do you call a dog that does magic tricks?

A: A labracadabrador.

Q: What do you call a slug on a boat?

A: A snailor.

Q: What did the bass say to the guitar when it was out of tune?

A: Don't fret about it!

Knock, knock.

Who's there?

Eureka.

Eureka who?

If Eureka shower may be in order!

Q: What do you call a stingray whose girlfriend broke up with him?

A: An ex-ray.

Q: What do you get when you cross a vampire and a boat?

A: A blood vessel!

Q: What's an astronaut's favorite dance?

A: The moonwalk.

Knock, knock.

Who's there?

Raisin.

Raisin who?

**Raisin your hand will get the teacher
to call on you.**

Knock, knock.

Who's there?

Llama.

Llama who?

Llama in, it's cold out here!

Knock, knock.

Who's there?

Wooden shoe.

Wooden shoe who?

Wooden shoe like to hear me tell another joke?

Q: What has a mouth but never eats?

A: A river.

Q: Why was the cow so hard to get along with?

A: Because it was moooo-dy!

Q: Why is Peter Pan always in the air?

A: Because he Neverlands!

Q: What kind of fish are good at poker?

A: Card sharks.

Q: Why don't clams share their toys?

A: They're shellfish!

Q: How do you know if your dentist went to college?

A: Read the plaque on her wall!

Q: What do you call a bug that's stubborn?

A: Belliger-ant!

Q: What do you get when you cross a dog and a table?

A: Fur-niture!

Knock, knock.

Who's there?

Wanda.

Wanda who?

Wanda hear another knock-knock joke?

HA HA
HA HA

Q: What did the vacuum say to the mop?

A: Don't mess with me!

Q: How do you know when a teakettle is upset?

A: When it's steaming.

Q: Why couldn't the butterfly go to the dance?

A: Because it was a mothball.

Q: Why do dragons sleep all day?

A: They're resting up for the knight.

Q: What's a frog's favorite snack?

A: French flies and diet croak.

Q: Why did the couple have their wedding at the carnival?

A: They wanted to ride the marry-go-round.

Q: What happened to the turkey when it got in a fight with the duck?

A: It got the stuffing knocked out of it.

Knock, knock.

Who's there?

There.

There who?

Don't you mean who's there?

**Q: What do sharks take when they
have a cold?**

A: Vitamin sea.

Knock, knock.

Who's there?

Acid.

Acid who?

Acid to open the door!

Q: **How do you get to the library on time?**

A: You book it!

Q: **Why don't tattoo artists sing soprano?**

A: Because it's piercing!

Q: **Why didn't anybody laugh at the fart joke?**

A: It just didn't cut it.

Q: **Why couldn't the fungus come in?**

A: There wasn't mushroom.

Q: What happened when the vampire went on a date?

A: It was love at first bite.

Q: What do you call a duck on the Fourth of July?

A: A firequacker!

Q: What do zombies serve at their tea parties?

A: Finger sandwiches.

**Q: Why should you never date a
  sausage?**

A: Because they're the wurst!

**Q: Why did the sheep keep waking
  up?**

A: It was having baaaaa-d dreams!

**Q: What did one llama say to the
  other llama?**

A: Alpaca basket for our picnic.

**Q: What did the mom dinosaur say to
  the baby dinosaur?**

A: Don't forget to fossil your teeth.

Q: Why do owls like knock-knock jokes?

A: They always know whoooo's there.

Q: How do you catch a school of fish?

A: With a bookworm.

Q: What don't mermaids catch the flu?

A: They use hand sand-itizer.

Q: Why did the author put on a sweater?

A: Because he was in the middle of a rough draft.

Q: What do you call a bug that's paying attention?

A: Observ-ant!

Q: What do turtles do in a downpour?

A: They run for shell-ter.

Q: Why couldn't the skeleton hold a job?

A: It was a deadbeat.

Q: Why did the student fail her cooking class?

A: She just couldn't measure up.

Knock, knock.

Who's there?

Wayne.

Wayne who?

The Wayne is really coming down, can you let me in?

Knock, knock.

Who's there?

Parmesan.

Parmesan who?

Do I have parmesan to come in?

Q: What do you call a potato at a football game?

A: A spec-tater.

Q: Why was the lightning mad?

A: Because someone stole his thunder!

Q: Why do snakes make great comedians?

A: Because they're hiss-terical.

Q: Why are peppers so annoying?

A: Because they always get jalapeño business!

Q: When is it hard to trust an artist?

A: When she's sketchy!

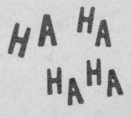

Q: **What did the horse do after the trail ride?**

A: It hit the hay.

Q: **What did the computer programmer do on her lunch break?**

A: She had a byte to eat.

Knock, knock.

Who's there?

Pizza.

Pizza who?

You'll get a pizza my mind if you don't open up!

- -

Q: What do a dog and a cell phone have in common?

A: They both have collar ID.

Q: Why did the clock get in trouble in class?

A: It wouldn't stop tocking.

Q: Why did the campers build a fire in the swamp?

A: They wanted to roast marsh-mallows.

Q: What is the best day of the week to go to the beach?

A: Sun-day!

Q: What did the lettuce say to the celery?

A: Quit stalking me!

Q: What's the coolest kind of vegetable?

A: A rad-ish!

Q: How can you tell if a joke is vegan?

A: It won't be cheesy.

Q: Why are pickles the most relaxing food in your refrigerator?

A: Because they're as cool as a cucumber.

Q: Where do tarantulas get their information?

A: From the worldwide web.

Jill: What's your favorite season?

Sue: Autumn.

Jill: Why is that?

Sue: Because it's beauti-fall.

Knock, knock.

Who's there?

Cash.

Cash who?

Bless you!

Knock, knock.

Who's there?

Mary.

Mary who?

Mary me someday?

Q: What kind of snake wants to come to your Thanksgiving dinner?

A: A pie-thon!

Q: Why did the boy lie down outside when it was raining?

A: He was under the weather.

Q: Why did the belt go to jail?

A: It held up a pair of pants.

Q: Why did the college student carry around a thermometer?

A: Because she wanted a degree.

Q: Why did the chef quit her job?

A: She was dish-illusioned.

Q: What is a gymnast's favorite dessert?

A: Banana splits!

Q: Why did King Arthur's parents ground him for a week?

A: Because he stayed out all knight.

Q: What did the leopard say after dinner?

A: "That hit the spot."

Knock, knock.

Who's there?

Highway.

Highway who?

Highway more now than I did before.

Knock, knock.

Who's there?

Jerky.

Jerky who?

Jerky doesn't work, so open the door!

Q: Why is a farmer such a good listener?

A: Because he'll always give you an ear.

Q: Why did the hen count her eggs?

A: Because she was a mathema-chicken!

Q: Why did the moon go to school?

A: It wanted to be as bright as the sun.

Q: What does a wasp sit on?

A: His bee-hind.

Q: Why did the cobra cross the road?

A: To get to the other sssssss-ide.

**Q: Why couldn't the wood fall asleep
in the dark?**

A: It was petrified.

Knock, knock.

Who's there?

Alexa.

Alexa who?

Alexa question when you open the door.

Q: What do you call it when your mom makes you wear a wrinkled shirt?

A: A cruel iron-y.

Mom: How did you hurt your arm?

Son: My shirt fell off the bed.

Mom: What does that have to do with it?

Son: I was wearing my shirt at the time!

Scott: I love geology!

Travis: Why?

Scott: Because my science teacher rocks!

Knock, knock.

Who's there?

Preston.

Preston who?

I Preston the doorbell, but nobody answered.

Q: What do you call a little old lady who goes south for the winter?

A: Migrate grandma!

Knock, knock.

Who's there?

Larva.

Larva who?

I larva you with all my heart!

Knock, knock.

Who's there?

Tolkein.

Tolkein who?

I'm Tolkein to you, OPEN UP!

Q: **Why did the tuna move to Hollywood?**

A: It wanted to be a starfish.

Q: **What do you get when you cross a chef and a meteorologist?**

A: Someone who knows how to cook up a storm!

Knock, knock.

Who's there?

Italy.

Italy who?

Italy a long time before I can come back to your house.

Q: **Why did the landscaper get the job?**

A: Because his work was cutting edge.

Emma: Did you hear about the guy whose freezer was stolen?

Anna: No, did they find the guy who took it?

Emma: No, the detective said it's a cold case.

Q: **What happened to the witch that broke her leg?**

A: She cast a spell.

Knock, knock.

Who's there?

Needle.

Needle who?

Needle little more time to open the door?

Q: What do you call a bunny that can fly?

A: A hare-icopter.

Q: Did you hear about the two snails that got in a fight?

A: They slugged it out until the end.

Q: What happened when the bakery closed?

A: It was dessert-ed.

Q: When do zombies like to come out and play?

A: In the dead of winter.

Q: Why did the man parachute off the windmill?

A: He was throwing caution to the wind!

Q: What do monsters wear in the winter to stay warm?

A: Cardi-goons.

Q: What position did the monster play in the soccer game?

A: The ghoulie.

Q: Why don't pilots eat sweets when they fly?

A: They're afraid of the sugar crash.

Knock, knock.

Who's there?

Nobel.

Nobel who?

You have Nobel, so I'm knocking.

- -

Q: What do you call a two-hundred-dollar steak at the butcher?

A: A raw deal.

Ted: Did you hear about the guy who got hit by lightning?

Tyler: No! Is he okay?

Ted: Yes! He had a shocking recovery!

Q: What did Shakespeare say when his teacher told him to get out his pencil?

A: "2B or not 2B?"

Q: Why did the noses break up?

A: They kept picking on each other.

Q: Why was the baker so brave?

A: She was one tough cookie!

Knock, knock.

Who's there?

Iran.

Iran who?

Iran all the way here!

Q: Why did the pony get in trouble?

A: It was horsing around.

Kristy: How do you like your

advanced math class?

Laura: It's as easy as pi.

Knock, knock.

Who's there?

Annie.

Annie who?

Annie thing you can do, I can do better!

Knock, knock.

Who's there?

Iguana.

Iguana who?

Iguana tell you another joke!

Q: What is a black belt's favorite drink?

A: Kara-tea.

Q: When do ducks get out of bed?

A: At the quack of dawn.

Q: Why did the baker get a new job?

A: He really kneaded the dough!

Q: What did the farmer do when he lost his dog?

A: He tractor down.

Q: What do you get if your feet fall asleep?

A: Coma-toes.

Knock, knock.

Who's there?

Candice.

Candice who?

Candice day get any better?

Q: How did the man learn to work at the railroad?

A: He got on-the-job train-ing.

Q: What is a lumberjack's favorite month?

A: Sep-timber!

Q: Why was the valley laughing?

A: Because the mountains were hill-arious!

Knock, knock.

Who's there?

Funnel.

Funnel who?

The funnel start once you open the door!

Q: What do cheerleaders eat for breakfast?

A: Cheerios.

Q: How does a skunk like to travel?

A: In a smell-icopter.

Girl: I'm afraid of that tree over there!

Dad: Don't worry, its bark is worse than its bite!

Q: Why did the girl take balloons to the show?

A: She heard it was a pop concert.

Q: What is a monster's favorite game?

A: Swallow the leader.

Q: How did the pirate feel when he found his buried treasure?

A: It was a weight off his chest!

Q: Why was the cheese sad?

A: It was blue cheese.

Q: **What do turtles like to do on vacation?**

A: Take a lot of shellfies.

Knock, knock.

Who's there?

Ireland.

Ireland who?

Ireland that I should call ahead next time!

Q: **Why was the dog purring like a kitten?**

A: It was taking a catnap.

Q: What do you call a sheep that does karate?

A: A lamb chop.

Q: What happened when the dog went to the vet?

A: It got a new leash on life!

Q: What do magicians like to eat after their show?

A: Pasta with presto sauce.

Knock, knock.

Who's there?

Pudding.

Pudding who?

Stop pudding me down!

Q: What do you get when you cross a laptop and a subway train?

A: A commuter.

Q: How do you know when your art teacher is upset?

A: He'll come unglued!

HA HA
HAHA

Q: What do you do when you have to walk your dog across the street?

A: Paws and look both ways before crossing!

Knock, knock.

Who's there?

Howard.

Howard who?

Howard you like to hear another knock-knock joke?

Q: Why do shrimp have 20/20 vision?

A: Because they're see-food.

Q: Why does the maid open all the windows when she cleans?

A: So it'll be a breeze.

Knock, knock.

Who's there?

Juicy.

Juicy who?

Juicy I'm at the door?

Q: What do horses like to eat for a snack?

A: Trail mix with hay-zelnuts!

Q: Why did the hornet fly back home?

A: He forgot his yellow jacket.

Q: Why did the vampire forget about Halloween?

A: He was going batty.

Knock, knock.

Who's there?

Colin.

Colin who?

I'm Colin you to hear another knock-knock joke.

Knock, knock.

Who's there?

Canteen.

Canteen who?

I'm canteen the minutes 'til you open the door!

Q: What did the golfer wear to the course?

A: His favorite tee-shirt!

Q: Why is it always so dark in an artist's house?

A: They like to keep the curtains drawn.

Q: How do lumberjacks go online?

A: They log in.

Q: Where does a swordfish like to play at the park?

A: On the sea-saw.

Q: What do you get when a butcher and a baker get married?

A: Meatloaf.

Knock, knock.

Who's there?

Radio.

Radio who?

Radio not, here we come!

Q: What do dogs like to eat for dinner?

A: Noodle cats-erole!

Q: Why don't cobras wear any clothes?

A: Because they're always snake-ed.

Q: What did the baker say when she picked a daisy?

A: He loaves me, he loaves me not . . .

Knock, knock.

Who's there?

Isabelle.

Isabelle who?

Isabelle working, or should I keep knocking?

Knock, knock.

Who's there?

Europe.

Europe who?

If Europe, please answer the door!

Q: Why was the shoe so happy?

A: It had found its sole mate.

Q: What is a skeleton's favorite instrument?

A: The organ.

Q: Where does a cow get its medicine?

A: From the farm-acy.

Q: Why did the chicken cross the road?

A: It was eggs-ploring.

Q: Why did the train conductor get a raise?

A: He had a good track record.

Knock, knock.

Who's there?

Ooze.

Ooze who?

Ooze in charge around here?

Knock, knock.

Who's there?

Hula.

Hula who?

Do you mean hula hoop?

Q: Why are Italian chefs so smart?

A: They know how to use their noodles!

Q: Why did the fisherman have a successful business?

A: He knew how to net-work.

Knock, knock.

Who's there?

Pacific.

Pacific who?

Be pacific so I know what you mean!

Q: What does soda pop wear when it's cold?

A: A bottle cap.

Q: How do you open the door of a haunted house?

A: With a spoo-key!

Q: Where do squirrels keep their nuts?

A: In the pan-tree.

Knock, knock.

Who's there?

Pasture.

Pasture who?

Pasture house and thought I'd stop and say hi.

Q: What do you get when you cross a cow and a Ferris wheel?

A: An a-moo-sement park!

Q: Why are sailors so adventurous?

A: They know how to seas the day!

Q: Where do monsters sleep when they come to visit?

A: In the ghost bedroom.

Q: What do you get from your dad on a hot day?

A: A pop-sicle!

Q: Did you hear about the doctor who became a comedian?

A: He'll keep you in stitches!

Knock, knock.

Who's there?

Towel.

Towel who?

Towel me how to unlock the door!

Knock, knock.

Who's there?

Prairie.

Prairie who?

I say a prairie every night before I go to sleep.

Q: Why did the scarecrow go back to school?

A: He wanted to work in a new field.

Knock, knock.

Who's there?

Dumpster.

Dumpster who?

She dumpster boyfriend so now she's single.

Q: Why was the peanut butter late for work?

A: There was a traffic jam.

HA HA
HAHA

Q: What's a mummy's favorite lunch?

A: A lettuce wrap.

Q: What do you call it when you burp

at the opera?

A: Embarras-sing!

Q: Why did the cow join a yoga class?

A: It wanted to be more flexi-bull!

Q: Why did the kid eat his boogers?

A: He was a picky eater.

Q: What happened when the banana store closed down?

A: There was no more monkey business!

Knock, knock.

Who's there?

Toucan.

Toucan who?

Toucan play at this game!

Knock, knock.

Who's there?

Fleas.

Fleas who?

Fleas open the door, it's cold outside.

Knock, knock.

Who's there?

Justin.

Justin who?

Justin time to hear another knock-knock joke!

Q: How do you catch a steelhead trout?

A: With a mag-net.

Q: What do a meteor and LeBron James have in common?

A: They're both shooting stars.

Knock, knock.

Who's there?

Jupiter.

Jupiter who?

Jupiter open the door before it's too late!

Knock, knock.

Who's there?

Shave.

Shave who?

I'll shave my jokes for when you open the door.

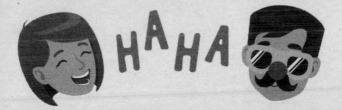

Q: **What is the best thing to read on a road trip?**

A: Car-toons!

Clarence: Do you like my underground fort?

Dan: Yeah, I dig it!

Q: **What did the blanket say to the bed?**

A: I've got you covered.

Q: How did the horse drink its water?

A: With its straw.

Knock, knock.

Who's there?

Mia.

Mia who?

Mia fingers hurt from knocking so much!

Q: What do you get when you cross an orange and a roller coaster?

A: Fruit loops!

Q: Why did the cookie go back to bed?

A: Because it felt crumby.

Leah: Did you hear about the skunk that wrote a book?

Lucero: Yes, it was a best-smeller!

Knock, knock.

Who's there?

Riley.

Riley who?

I Riley want you to open up!

Q: What kind of bug works for the CIA?

A: A spy-der!

Q: What language do birds speak?

A: Portu-geese.

Q: What did the sailor do when he was feeling sick?

A: He went to see the dock.

Q: Why did the lion jump in the lake?

A: It wanted to be a bobcat.

Knock, knock.

Who's there?

Gopher.

Gopher who?

Gopher a walk with me today?

Q: Why do bakers make good actors?

A: They can play any kind of roll.

**Mom: How do you feel about visiting
the farm today?**

Girl: I'm on pens and needles!

Knock, knock.

Who's there?

Razor.

Razor who?

Razor hand before you ask a question.

Knock, knock.

Who's there?

Mustache.

Mustache who?

I mustache if you like my jokes.

Q: Why did the police take a picture of the coffee cup?

A: They needed a mug shot.

Knock, knock.

Who's there?

Donkey.

Donkey who?

This donkey won't open the door!

Q: What do astronauts use to clean their rockets?

A: Comet.

HA HA
HA HA

Knock, knock.

Who's there?

Garbage can.

Garbage can who?

Garbage can really stink if you don't take it out.

Q: Why did Smokey the Bear go on vacation?

A: For-rest!

Knock, knock.

Who's there?

Luke.

Luke who?

Luke out the window and you'll see!

Knock, knock.

Who's there?

Feud.

Feud who?

Feud open the door, I could tell you another knock-knock joke!

Q: What do you call a girl bug?

A: A flea-male.

Knock, knock.

Who's there?

Narnia.

Narnia who?

It's Narnia business!

Q: How does a composer travel to the opera?

A: In the Bach seat!

Knock, knock.

Who's there?

Thor.

Thor who?

I'm Thor from knocking so much!

Q: Where do soldiers keep their uniforms?

A: In the war-drobe.

Knock, knock.

Who's there?

Axe.

Axe who?

Axe me no questions, I'll tell you no lies.

Q: How do starfish pay for their food?

A: With their sand dollars.

Q: How do you get a chef to speed up in the kitchen?

A: Tell her to chop chop!

Mummy: Did Casper write that book himself?

Werewolf: No, he used a ghost writer.

Knock, knock.

Who's there?

Snowman.

Snowman who?

Snowman is an island.

Q: What's a sandwich's favorite song?

A: "For he's a jelly good fellow."

Q: What do you get when you cross a bird and a werewolf?

A: A h-owl.

Knock, knock.

Who's there?

Oil change.

Oil change who?

Oil change my socks in the morning.

Q: What do greyhounds like to put in their coffee?

A: Whippet cream!

What do you call a gullible panda?

Bamboo-zled!

Q: What do you get if you give a panda some dynamite?

A: Bamboom!

Q: Why did the farmer use a dating app?

A: He wanted a relation-sheep.

Knock, knock.

Who's there?

Nacho.

Nacho who?

I'm nacho if you're going to let me in!

Knock, knock.

Who's there?

Alligator.

Alligator who?

Alligator a few more knock-knock jokes.

Q: What does a lumberjack say when he's cold?

A: Timbrrrrrr!

Q: Who's in charge at the furniture factory?

A: The chairman!

Q: What did the python wear to the party?

A: A boa tie.

Knock, knock.

Who's there?

Patty-cake.

Patty-cake who?

Patty-cake on the table so everybody can have some.

Sammy: Can I tell you about my new underwear?

Jimmy: Well, keep it brief.

Q: What happens when green grapes hold their breath?

A: They turn purple.

Knock, knock.

Who's there?

Dishes.

Dishes who?

Dishes my last joke for this book!